Bright Side
of Life

Live. Love. Inspire.

EDITED AND COMPILED BY-
CHETAN BATRA

Bright Side Of Life
© 2020

ISBN 9781648289392

First Edition 2020

This book is dedicated–
To all the people living in a black hole,
cheer up life is beautiful

Special Thanks to–
Mankaran Singh
Shubham Singh
Anjali Jha

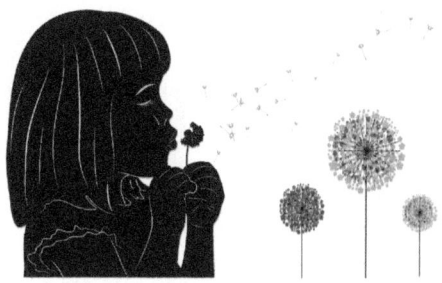

Dear Stranger,

Feel confident about the things you have achieved till now. I know, its been a wild ride going through lot of upheavals. Don't care about what you have done, even if you did mistakes it hardly matters. Everyone does mistakes, its a common phenomena but we insist on making it complicated and think, 'I should have not done this'.

Leave it buddy, these things doesn't matter us anymore. You need to think very much different, gone are the days when we used to mock your choices. Life is not a choice, its always a next time. Your mind is a powerful thing, fill it with positive thoughts as you move on you will start feeling a change that matters. Bury your burden of negative thoughts, and make this world a better place to live and feel proud for.

Try to live in your own joy just like this girl blowing dandelion. There is always something to live and cherish on.
Simple thoughts admire destiny...

God Bless You Always

ACKNOWLEDGEMENTS

I would like my express special thanks of gratitude to all the contributing writers without you all this project would have been impossible.

I visualized a dream one year back, a dream to collaborate with 42 brilliant writers of the country. My dream has finally come true, I highly appreciate the sincere honesty of the writers and their patience throughout the publishing journey of this anthology.

A special vote of thanks to my family for their constant support.

My heart felt appreciation to my Author friend Shubham Singh, your contribution to the book is invaluable and special thanks to you for the particular quote for the book blurb.

My sincere prayers to God, who looks after me.

Last but not the least, to the readers, for picking up the book and making it a comfortable companion.

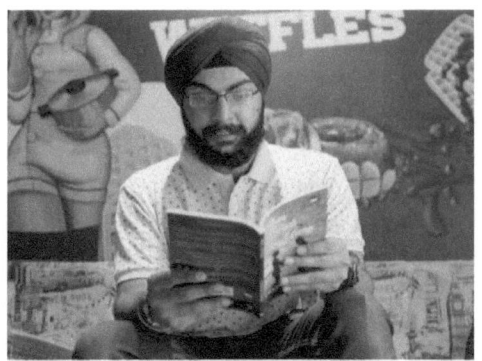

<u>EDITER AND COMPILER</u>
CHETAN BATRA

Chetan Batra is a law graduate, poet, blogger, and writer born and raised in Ludhiana, Punjab. 23-year old Chetan has a keen interest in crime fiction. Apart from writing he is big fan of Bollywood and holds an extravagant dream to try his luck in film-making. His latest book titled, 'Never Fade Away', got released last year and received rave reviews from the readers.

Chetan is a true believer of destiny and always inspire the people to opine the positive side of life.
You can connect with Chetan via-
Facebook-
www.facebook.com/achetan.batra
Instagram- @achetanbatra
Email- chetan972@gmail.com

INDEX

Quotes, Poems, Thoughts and Short Stories

1. Shubham Singh   1
2. Sakshi Arora   3
3. Sanjana Sankhyan   6
4. Rajat Joshi   9
5. Mankaran Singh   10
6. Suryansh S. Chauhan   11
7. Chetan Batra   13
8. Anjali Jha   17
9. Vishal Tekade   20
10. Kaandeeban Mohanraj   21
11. Kriti Sood   22
12. Kanak Lata Sharma   23
13. Yasmin Khan   25
14. Mona Dokania   27
15. Priya Nayer   29
16. Rimjhim Chandrakant   32
17. Areeba Ashraf   34
18. Priyanka Vegda   36
19. Sunita Jash   37
20. Varsha Saxena   39
21. Anuj   41
22. Raghu Mahendru   43
23. Mohamed Faizal   44
24. Tamanna Mohapatra   47
25. Sonali Sharma   49
26. Vivek Marwaha   51
27. Baman Tadiwala   52
28. Prathna Das   53
29. Himanshu Leekha   56

30. Amandeep Verma   57
31. Dashmesh Saini   58
32. Lovie Matharoo   60
33. Anjali Kashyap   61
34. Priyanshi Mussadi   62
35. Shruti Tayal   64
36. Bikram Chowdhury   66
37. Aaradhana Agarwal   68
38. Geetanshi Muttreja   71
39. Lavisha   73
40. Muskan Goel   75
41. Danica Rayen   76
42. Sabi Shaikh   78

Bios of Writers

1. Mankaran and Sanjana   81
2. Suryansh S. and Vishal   82
3. Kandeeban M. and Kanak   83
4. Mona and Priyanka   84
5. Varsha and Mohamed   85
6. Sonali and Vivek   86
7. Areeba and Prathna Das   87
8. Dashmesh, Priya and Baman   88
9. Shruti Tayal and Bikram   89
10. Aradhana and Geetanshi   90
11. Anjali and Kriti Sood   91
12. Amandeep and Tamanna   92
13. Himanshu and Anuj   93
14. Raghu and Muskan Goel   94
15. Sakshi and Priyanshi   95
16. Shubham and Rimjhim   96
17. Sunita Josh and Anjali   97
18. Yasmin Khan and Danica   98

19. Lavisha and Rajat Joshi   99
20. Sabi Shaikh and Lovie M.   100

Shubham Singh
Prayagraj, U.P.

Instagram ID– livesimplicite

1. Student: "What are the consequences of knowing and following our legend?"

Guide: "Those who never had any dream, will ridicule you. Those who never failed, because they never took any risk, will fill you with fears of 'being different.' Those who themselves want what you are trying to achieve, but never had the courage to act, will call you arrogant and selfish. Those who share the same direction as you, will inspire you and take inspiration from you. Those who are concerned for you, will want you to be safe. But those who love you, will say, "I believe in God, and I believe in you."

2. Student: "How does one demean oneself?"

Guide: "One does not demean oneself by not doing good, but one does when one knows what's good and stands for the wrong. One does not demean oneself by not praying, but one does when one does not seek joy. One does not demean oneself by not giving, but one does when one gives selfishly. One does not demean oneself when one loses in love, but one does when, after losing in love, one fights for possession. And finally, one does not demean oneself by not trying to please God, but one does when one tries to please others."

3. Student: "How can we be extraordinary?"

Guide: "By being simple, and by working hard. Not by trying to stand-out, but by willing to out stand every obstacle. By getting-up after falling, and not by not falling at all. By hoping to gain something after investing something. By believing in luck without testing it. By accepting the blessings without being greedy. Not by pointing at the world, but by pointing in the mirror.

"Extraordinary is not an ordinary who did extra. Extraordinary is an ordinary who tried extra."

Sakshi Arora
Prayagraj, U.P.

Instagram ID – sakshiarora8467

1. Blackout

In the cold and mysteriously beautiful
night,
Admist the starry mates,
The pale moon gleams and spreads
dazzling light
Sighs within. Strange fate!

Crowd of ally and the mechanical
laughing sound
Admist the known pals,
Still heart sinks and the loneliness
bound
Peace of heart falls.

Forlorn in the crowd,
Content being alone.
Sunny in solitude,
Admist the crowd, the cold heart
moans.

When the world around is cold and
black,
You cheerfully be intact.
Admist the calculated people, harmony
lacks
Spread warmth, accepting sour facts.

2. Pure Love

Wick! Why you consume every-time and
let the candle glow?

Do you abhor yourself or you feel low?
No. I can elucidate, why I do so.
Why I want my candle to grow.

I do not detest myself but I love the
candle more
I cannot see him burning in pain and
simply roar.
To his ache, I can't just shut the door
Love is more than these letters four.

If my blazing can lighten up his soul
If my sacrifices can fulfill his goal.
If my duties can uphold his role
I will again drain myself whole.

Love is to give, not to take
It's to be happy for your lover's sake.
The bliss is pure, not fake
That's how bonds we make.

I realized why this wick burns
Now it's your turn.
Do comprehend and learn.
Love is never snatched, it's always
won.

3. Mingled Love

Mix like the salt in water
How beautiful! I ponder.
Interweave like the strips of straw
Amusingly, I awe.

Blend like the hues in a canvas
How splendid! I guess.
Embrace like the farrago of emotions
Perfect! the only notion.

Loved and souls met.
Pure! I bet.
Wrapped and hearts unified
Here is the love and light.

Merge like the confluence of seas
Soothing as the gentle breeze.
Hook up like the water that mix
perfectly,
Don't meet like two oceans that never
intermix completely.

Sanjana Sankhyan
Ludhiana, Punjab

Instagram ID – ssanjana16

1. Learn To Live Alone

Nobody cares about nobody. Everybody's busy making their own grass greener. Never expect people to water your gardens. They're never going to do that. You have to learn to live alone. All alone.
Expectations will hurt you in end. Even the best ones in your life will disappoint you. Nobody will ever understand your happiness, your sorrows, your needs and your perspective. They'll never bother about you unless and until they have their own selfish reasons behind it. You came into this world alone, and you'll be going out all alone. Accept yourself as you are and stop throwing your happiness in someone's else basket, because honey they are going to drop it every single time.

2. Make Your-Self Happy

Everyone wants to be happy, yet joy is elusive for most people. One reason is that people tend to expect their happiness to come from big things. To have a truly happy, peaceful existence, however it is necessary to find happiness in little things. Life is made up of little things, so enjoying them for all their worth is bound to make for a more pleasant life. Being happy content with the small in life requires us to slow down and take time to enjoy those pretty little things in life.

Slow down enough to sit with your animal friend and show it a bit of affection. Playing a simple board game can also ring off your house with laughter. You don't always need a plan, sometimes you just need to breath and do what your heart demands, maybe that's what happiness is.

For most of the life nothing wonderful happens. If you don't enjoy getting up and working and finishing your work and sitting down to a meal with family or friends, then chances are that you're not gonna be very happy. Just try playing with a child, trust me it gives you so much joy. These little things add up to your happiness, they'll one day become beautiful memories. Your happiness depends on only and only you. So, try doing things for yourself, to make yourself happy. Don't run for great goals that might give you joy in future, instead find your present day happiness in small little things.

3. Keep on Believing

Believe, that no matter what happens, or how bad it seems today, life does go on and it will get better tomorrow.

Believe, that regardless of your relationship with your parents you'll miss them when they are gone. Believe, that people can change and it is okay for them to change. Believe, that whenever you decide something with open hearts, you always decide the best. Believe that you still have a lot memories to make. Believe that you have a lot more to learn. Believe that people will forget what you did, and that expectations will hurt you. Believe that life will never give you second chances. Believe that begging someone to love you will not work. Believe that this is life and it goes on no matter what.

Rajat Joshi
Hoshiarpur, Punjab

Instagram ID – _darkershade_

1. Rise up

So, look up and take the less taken
road,
And rise, rise and make the sky your
abode.
Work harder everyday, unleash the
beast mode.
You fight your battles alone,
You're worthy, you wield the sword..!!

2. Eyes

Eyes may cry,
As the night goes on.
Heart might want to give up,
With no signs of dawn.
And for a ray of light,
Your soul you'd want to pawn.

That's when you shall remember,
It is okay to cry and let your tears fall.
You won't even know,
When from the darkness, the light will
crawl.
The night to pain and despair may
seem to last for ever,
But remember, no matter how long or
dark it is, it is just a night after all.

Mankaran Singh
Ludhiana, Punjab

Instagram ID- kathuria.ms

1. The best way to live an optimistic life is by grabbing the positive opportunity from a negative mindset.

2. Misunderstandings are the biggest barriers to successful life. Clear the misunderstandings before it clears the scarf.

3. Life is all about taking risks, setting new challenges and doing what's impossible.

Suryansh S. Chauhan
Kota, Rajasthan

Instagram ID – suryansh_s_chauhan

1. Champion

It's only the beginning,
and I'm miles away from winning.
The way is long, it'll buffer
Pain is on the way.
And I'm ready to suffer,
each and everyday.
Tied my shoelace,
I'm ready for the race.
I'm prepared for loss too,
you know, just in case.
It takes years of hard-work,
A champion isn't prepared in a matter
of days.
I'll go beyond the limits,
hit the wickets
Stadium full of people,
sold out all tickets.
Thousands of people cheering my
name,
And I'm standing strong focusing on my
game.
All my sweat, all my blood shall pay
back as my success & my fame.

2. Miles to walk before I sleep

Ain't this one another long journey?
Haven't you suffered like this before?
Miles to walk before I sleep,
I'll have to stand strong therefore.

Bright Side of Life

Looking outta the window,
Tons of fascinating scenarios.
And I've found an escape,
While my eyes are working like a
videotape.
When people are into their phones,
I'm embracing the nature.

Elevating mountains, emanating rivers
on the way,
while traveling through contrary zones.
Maybe I've fallen in love with myself,
or maybe I'm going insane with the flow.
Miles to walk before I sleep,
So here I go!

Chetan Batra
Ludhiana, Punjab

Instagram ID – achetanbatra

1. Over-thinking

I hear a world of disappointment, I hear state of things that proven to be doubtful to its existence. All day the young mind try to endure its limitations and toil-worn the positive attitude. It takes much power, strength, time, efforts to make one impact and we take no time to destroy it due to overthinking.

I know you feel ashamed, being imprisoned with obsessive over-thinking thoughts. The only key to unlock the prison is when you rise up and attack the sight with great energy and enthusiasm.

There is nothing so dangerous in the world as much as your own thoughts. Overthinking corrupts our potential, don't give the mind chances to over-think again and again, it creates more problems that were even there in first stance. Never give your mind a reason to hate yourself, you need to change your thoughts to change your life.

Imagine a world full of life, a world full of reality, a world dealing with positive energies. Try to overcome bad impeaches, kill the negatives thoughts for positive emotions. The picture of overthinking is the most screwing part of life; rise up and do what is good for your soul, do what heals you within.

'Don't let the negative thoughts to control your life. Stay positive. Stay strong.'

2. When Fear Knocks

He knocked the door and repeated the words, 'Hey.. let me come in. I promise you I will not hurt you this time'.

'No', I shouted

'Chetan, please understand will not hurt you, I am here to help you', he repented

I was too afraid to open the door. I meted to walk away from my fear, he knocked again. 'Chetan.. please open the door'. He constantly peeved in and tried to unlock the door. I was feeling suffocated in this odd environment. I looked at the door and turned my head away in disappointment, irritating with this on-going life. I wasn't going through smoothly, wailing at my choices. I was unable to take a stand, almost living a half life. I was scared been knocked down by fear 3 times, and again he is knocking my house door with a promise that I will not hurt you again. I was in a fix to make a different choice or let him break-in again. I held my head high, with a cool temper I confronted myself in front of a mirror.

'To be or not to be'

I waited down myself for past own hour, and I finally made a decision. Let him come in, and will show him the real me. I will make him realize–
The real strength lies inside a person, no matter how big the fear is. Let your real strength confront him, and show them how strong you are....

'When fear knocks on the door again and again to disappoint you. Send your valued strength to answer it.'

3. Fight Alone

I am good in my own, I care about things that really matters to me. I start on the things with a hope that new beginnings do bring out the best in me.
Somehow, I feel suffocated about past illusions driving my new future. The matter of fact is that past mistakes pinches down future prospects every time I try to make a move. It itches my soul, been taking on the things for granted. These illusions are nothing but gamble cards turning the right things to wrong.
No one can help you in this, you need to be strong to fight alone. Whatever your life gives you, no matter what happens, you can always choose to be strong and turn the things in your favor. You are the master of your time, you lone need to be the knight in shining armor to protect life.

'Say goodbye to past today for a better tomorrow. If anything hurts you, do what serves good to you.'

Anjali Jha
Darbhanga, Bihar

Instagram ID – anjalikumarjha

1. Never Give Up

Life is strange with twists and turns,
But you must have to learn,
Sometimes things may go wrong as you
never want,
Sometimes everything may be against
you,
You will find a bunch of problems,
But never give up in your life.
Sometimes funds will be low and debts
will be high,
But you have to smile and you have to
sigh,
Sometimes, someone's care will be
pressed you down a bit,
But you must have to move forward,
And never give up in your life.
Success is not final and failure is not
fatal,
But you have to work hard,
Your dreams are never ending,
And they are not few at any point,
So stop wasting your time anymore,
And never give up in your life.
There is so much you have to do,
Don't sit behind with folded hands any
more,
Don't blame always to your destiny,
Your destiny is always in your hand,
One day you will get all what you want to
find,
So, never give in your life.
Brand new opportunities are knocking
your door,

Get up, walk outside and start moving
towards goals,

Don't look back what you did and who are
with you,
Don't be scared even if your ideas are
failed sometimes,
I know you have the capability to make
your dreams come true,
So never give up in your life.
You are the creator of your destiny,
You are the inspiration of many,
Why are you feeling down,
People will come and go from life,
Only few can live in your side,
Never give up in your life.
Your goal is nearer than your thoughts,
Only you have to grab as soon as you
can,
Athletes run several on the track,
But only few win in the race,
Those who can continue on the track,
So, never give up in your life.

2. Life is so Complicated

Life is a surprise
It can amaze you
Bring abrupt changes and twists
But life is just a joyful ride
For the one who with these experience
learn
A dream, an ambition, it is all attainable
All you need to do, is believe in yourself
A hope, some faith, will find it's way,
All you need is an eye, to perceive it.
Life is a twisted road dominated
somewhere
By unexpected twists and turns
However at the end of the day,

It is from them that we learn everything
In-spite of being so hard to cross
barriers
The flame of hope ensures that you're
never lost
So keep the flame of hope inside yourself,
Always bright and strong inside yourself.
Life is very tough
Life gives you sorrow and pain
But you will learn and you will gain,
Life is unexpected and it will change
Things will change with time
Everything will be okay just wait for the
time.
Life is very complicated
We often lose our say,
Things become really tough
That we often lose our way.
Life is our friend
We can't fake it and pretend
When it hits us hard,
We have to find a solution
We have to find our own way.
Life is so complicated at somewhere
Nothing is simple and untangled anymore
Nothing is as it seems from outside,
Always there is a puzzle inside it
Always waiting to grab you when you
least expected it to.
Nothing can be accomplished without
complications
All you have to do to solve it's puzzle,
Life is so complicated
And all you have to unravel it's
complications.

Vishal Tekade
Nagpur, Maharastra

Instagram ID – vishal.tekade

1. Every impossibility walks with
possibility,
Every failure walks with success,
Every disadvantage walks with
advantage,
Every weakness walks with strength
But to see it,
One needs vision not only eyes.

2. Success is not about what you
achieve,
Success is how you live,
No matter what you achieve.

3. The only constructor of limited-legs
and limitless-legs is your
'Commitment'.

Kaandeeban Mohanraj
Karaikal, Pondicherry

Instagram ID – kaandeeban_mohanraj

1. When the world gives you no chances, don't fall but make yours.

2. People are always remembered by the rest. Its your family or the whole world decides whether you are ordinary or beyond that.

3. Make enemies wish you bad luck so that you could prove their gods you are unstoppable.

Kriti Sood
Ludhiana, Punjab

Instagram ID– ksood036

1. Your first inspiration is your final destination.

2. Inspiration has no expiration.

3. Inspiration does not come with looks, "Just look at your books".

Kanak Lata Sharma
Ghazipur, U.P.

Instagram ID – nutan___Sharma

1. World We Live In

Don't know which world I live in,
Perhaps, with a dream in mind,
I fly in anticipation,
Beyond every world, hoping for a
destination,
Probably, on the staggering path, she
went flying.
With no mind in mind, regardless of
success
Seeing that the wings went flying.
Don't know which world I live in,
Probably beyond the people, in a poem,
In a remote settlement,
There is a girl who walks up stairs,
With a hope in heart, a thirst for
success,
Wanting diamonds, now on the way to
gold,
Look, that girl flew away.
Beyond the world, with bird's wings,
Seeing that girl flew away.
Look behind the passion,
She went away,
With pen in hands, love in Heart,
Look, that girl flew away.
To dream of climbing the dream,
Neither did the world flow,
Built a dream house
Seeing that girl flew away..

2. It's My Life

It's my life, It's my future
Who are you to interfere
O god.! I seek inside with
Fear and challenges outside.
Talent and thoughts given by you
makes me unique.
O god please understand my feelings.
Please show me your honesty and love,
Guide me to be a good speaker.
O god O god.....
You are powerful, you are doctor of the
world..
Tell me why and why our mother is
suffering yes our mother earth.
Tell me why?
Oh I wish if I could meet you my life
I know who ever meet you will never
come back.
But, today the world forces each and
every suffering people to come to meet
you forever.
Oh god... Oh god...
By heart, I am telling, I wish if I could
I know you are magician,
You can know and I know,
You know...

Yasmin Khan
Pondicherry

Instagram ID – dark_artist _._

1. The Art of Love

Long years of my wait didn't go in vain,
After spotting a soul that can share
both my bliss and pain.
I neither had the map nor knew the way
to reach you my destination,
But God has fixed us both together
before the creation.
I have left my universe behind to live
with you,
Never replace me for indeed I am born
for you.
All the bonds in the universe might fade,
But the bond we shared will never and
would glide through the shade.
The sigh of yours made me feel
breathless,
The presence of yours have made me
bit reckless.
Find me please for I am lost within you,
Leave me not for I am immersed in you.

2. The Art of Eye–Lock

Nothing strikes me at times,
For your eyes mingles with mine forcing
me to go blank.
No words can match at times,
Seeing your lopsided smile making me
go flatter.

3. Vicinity of Life

The roses wilted. Yes, your roses wilted.
Look at it, accept and bid a bye to it
instead of placing it in between your
favourite book. Stop fooling yourself
that it'd come back to life just because
you loved it
much more than anyone and anything
and that its mere presence would paint
away your worries into a happy picture.
No, it won't. So bid a bye to the rose
and store it not in the pages of your
book or in your garden or in your vicinity
of life. Not all roses are yours and not
all your roses stay yours.

Every rose has its timing to stay.
Respect and let it stay. When its stay is
over, don't plead it to stay. Just see the
pink sky and wave a smile. Everything
happens for a reason. Even a sudden
breakup.

Mona Dokania
Gurgaon, Haryana

Instagram ID – beauty_of_thou_words

1. Beautiful

Will you still call me Beautiful?
If I make you hear the silence
Of A broken heart in those
Pounding beats.
If I show you the Wounded soul
Refusing to deck up hair,
And those dead dried lips
With a Name burning on my tongue.
If I remove the Silken drape,
To Expose those Naked scars and
Bleeding cuts.
Will you still call me Soulful?
If you see the strong winds caged
within
Tearing the skies, uprooting the
Emotions.
If I reveal the Smudged Remains
Of his heart in my broken fragments.
If u see the lies falling from
The corners of my eyes.
Will you still call me a beautiful soul?
If I Show you the shameless touch
Rolling on me, with a promise
To be my love for an Eternity.

2. Cursed Soul

Beneath the crepuscular sky,
The irradiating Silhouette Babbles,
O'Lady

Taste the Sin of the Cursed Beauty,
Thou Starving for ages,
Stripping off the Infinite darkness.
Moldering the dreams, in the
Sugarcoated Myths
of the Canonical verity,
Thou being the epitome of Carnality
decked within.
Plunge into the Agony of Barbarous
fate,
Succumbing to the raging flames.
O'Lady
There you are shuddering, to the
domineering
Nefarious Mankind.
Festering the Rots Further In the body,
Dethroned, with those Bruised wings
Awaiting the ashes of pyres to fade
away,
Emancipating your scintillating
Panache,
Behind the dripping ink,
painting the tattered pages,
demolishing the Dominance
of the Abhorrent Coterie.
O'Lady
Darn your shredded soul,
Metamorphosing the shambles, you are
Behind the Endless saga of the beauty
you uphold within.

Priya Nayer
Prayagraj, U.P.

1. You're No Less

Countless of people but issue is one
Who here's greater and who has more
fun
In race of comparison, endlessly you
run
Sleepless nights lit up by the rising sun
They may be happier, you may be a
mess
But in spreading happiness you're no
less.
Skin colour may be white, or may be
black
But in any case, your beauty doesn't
lack
Soul may be black, or it may be white
But if it's the former, unholy is your
sight
They may be prettier, you may be a
mess
But in your pretty smile, you're no less.
They may have won, you may have lost
A person or a goal, either be the cost
Believing in yourself is what you choose
Then in love or in life, you can't ever
lose
They may have done, you may be a
mess
But in selfless commitment you're no
less.
They may be born with a lot more
wealth
Not being jealous keeps good your
health

Ask for his blessings, not for more cash
Or your greedy fire will burn you to ash
They may be richer, you may be a mess
But in your rich thoughts, you're no less.
Life may have turned to a pathetic
state
Constant struggle may now be your
fate
If your plan to give up becomes a
history
Then all's left is just you and your
victory
They may be easy, you may be a mess
But to win in hard times, you're no less.

2. Your Sun Will Rise

The sun is seen a number of times
At times it fades and at times it shines
Life is a sun burning high in tests
Tests of pains and tears and rest.
Despite the fears, the failures, the lies
You will smile back and your sun will rise

Every leaf sheds and a new comes out
Every life is tough, this fact you dare
not doubt
Every soul is tired and has continually
fought
With thoughts that aren't reality, reality
that isn't thought.
Despite you sink, drink, overthink really
nice
You will smile back and your sun will
rise.

The sun dries up both ocean and lakes
Weak or strong, everyone's heart
breaks

Each morning that smile that you take
Will soon become real,which today you
fake
Despite the void,the screams,the cries
You will smile back and your sun will
rise.

Darkest nights bring the brightest light
Hold on to persistence with all your
might
Surely you'll cross all the negative vibes
Beyond hopelessness lies the brighter
side of life.
Despite the burning sun, every bird flies
You will smile back, and your sun will
rise.

Rimjhim Chandrakant
Prayagraj, U.P.

Instagram ID – rim.jhim_31

An Ode to Life

You are asked: to shine bright like a
diamond,
But you decide: to burn effulgent like a
coal.
Their opinion won't be a reality –
Be Herculean and endure their troll.
Life's a journey, and we're mere
travelers covering miles,
Life do offer hardships, whether you're
old or juvenile.
Do the undone task and make your mark
permanent:
I've been told by someone, to just keep
chasing my Legend.
Never ever you dare, to welcome
atrocity and
sorrow,
The obstacles faced today, are
gateways of tomorrow.
Life's a challenge: Meet it.
Life's a duty: Complete it.
Life's a song: Sing it.
Life's a struggle: Keep it.
Keep the valour constant, and put plans
in motion,
As tiny drops of water, make a mighty
ocean.
This little kingdom of yours might never
achieve fame,

Count your blessings: it's not always
about the name.
Now that you know that life's not so
mean,
It is never late to be what you might
have been.
If you're a champion you have to have it
in your heart,
Gear up your life; I hope you have a
good start.

Areeba Ashraf
Sitapur, U.P.

Instagram ID – tanyaashraf123

1. Alone

Alone you were, coming into this world,
Alone you will be leaving this world.
You will own it all on your own girl,
You don't need anyone to give you a hurl.
No, you need no one to love you,
You are enough to love yourself.
Times are tough, situations are tough ,
But you are tougher to break.
You don't need to think about what people will say,
Girl you just have to "slay".
You don't need anyone by your side,
You just need to hold your ambitions tight.

If you have thoughts bittersweet,
Go give yourself a warm treat.
You don't need a king,
You yourself are a very powerful being.
You have to stand for yourself in this vast ocean,
So hold your emotions,
And do your actions.
Alone you were, coming into this world,
Alone you will be leaving this world.

2. Wings

You don't see them,
But you have them.

They are with you by birth,
To explore this beautiful earth.
At first people praise them,
But after sometime they try to erase
them,
But you have to embrace them, so that
no one can efface them.
Spread them as wide as you can,
And fly as high as you can.
Make them shine so bright,
That everyone love to see your sight.
No one can tell you how wide your
wingspan should be,
No one can tell you what you shouldn't
be.
So brush your feathers,
And be the inspiration for others.

3. Your Never Walk Alone

When you feel low sometimes, don't
want to talk with anyone, don't want to
interact with anyone.
That's when you think that you are done
with this world, and you forget that
there is more than that in this world.
When you feel low, go have a walk at a
place quiet and slow.
When you feel like talking to nobody, but
still you want to share it with somebody,
then talk with yourself, share with
yourself, because you are the best gift
to yourself.
Give some alone time to yourself, love
yourself, discover yourself, and be the
best friend with yourself.
Surely you will discover some new
things about yourself, when you will
have a good walk with yourself.

Priyanka Vegda
Mumbai, Maharastra

Instagram ID- priyanka_vegda

1. Everyone wants that one person to
support in good or bad,
To cry out or laugh louder whenever
happy or sad.

2. The best things in life are when you
expect something good to happen and
that turn out to be better.

3. You left me alone, you left me
broken,
You broke my trust and made me shock
and shaken.
It's just that my mind will forget the pain
but my scars won't,
In my hard times, I needed you the most,
my heart will forgive but my scars
won't.

Sunita Jash
Kolkata, West Bengal

Love You Zindagi

We, the earthly simple human beings are too stupid to expect from others, always. An extra chocolate from our teacher for good marks, a long drive with our best friend for enjoying the beach side view while sunset, a smooch from the spouse or the partner to remind that he or she is the special one. All these indicate that we are somehow searching betterment through our expectations.

Lord Buddha said that expectations are the key to sorrow. But we can feel that expectations are also the key to live in this earth.

So contradicting, right?

The mother, expecting her baby, cherishes herself everyday, rather every moment with a new dream, a newer info, the newest anxiety. The writer engulfs whatever he experiences and expects to garnish his write ups with those delicate realizations. The farmer expects to harvest the crops after the toiling days and sweating waits. We should keep ourselves in the pace to achieve our expectations. Just expect from yourself, and Nature Earth, not from any other individual–not even from your parents, your spouse or partner, your children, simply none: Just from yourself.

Have you ever noticed the mountain rill? The stones and rocks which harden her route, she washes away them silently to meet her destiny. She never expects for a miracle or an earthquake to remove those obstacles. She believes herself only. She soothes herself in breeze, brightens herself in the sun, brims herself to the fullest in the rain, mystifies herself in the moonbeam, and makes her own way in her own terms.

It is the only you who feeds you, teaches you, makes you happy, wets eyes in sorrow. You are the one who is always protecting and grooming you, keeping you, loving you, be with you in darkness as well as in limelight.

Sing the songs though you have no melody in your voice, colour the canvas even if you aren't an artist, experience the movies alone in the theatre, go to the restaurants only with your filled wallet and empty stomach, walk alone through the roads by gazing surroundings. Enjoy the chilled winter evenings in the rooftop with your favourite sound track, or spend the nights with your favourite novel. Give time to your hobbies, fertilize your well-being.

So inspire yourself, make yourself happy, scold yourself, correct yourself, nourish yourself, cherish yourself, and finally expect, only from yourself.

Varsha Saxena
Lucknow, U.P.

Instagram ID – varsha_writes

1. Thousands of Masks

Shedding thousands of masks
Floating all over my face,
Was the very first step
To leave this pace.
I tried really hard
To cover my tracks
Sealed my lips
For the truth unheard.
I was down in the dumps
With a sinking heart,
Almost died in a way
None can imagine, even a part.
I was walking there
Being all alone,
Suddenly,
Reached the crossroads
Stopped thinking
About my own.
Is this the way I always wanted?
Is this the way
To my lost dreams?
No.. I shed the skin
So tight on me,
Let all the masks
Go away in the sea.
I let all the tears
Fall from my heart
To lead the way,
To a new life's start.

2. An Introvert– Closed Self

The home in me, shrinks
And the door closed so tight,
These days are passing
And it still seems to me as night.
People love substances,
I love one's soul;
Things are so materialistic
Rather being love for all.
This home seems good
It's full of pain!
But just for once,
I don't want to live in vain.

Anuj Arjun
New Delhi

Instagram ID – anuj.vats.79

God Bless Your Eyes

God bless your eyes
for looking at me
the way you look at me.
I can see myself
in your eyes
when you see me.
Being more honest,
I can see more than myself.
I can see what I can be more.
I can see where I am wrong.
Just seeing myself
in your eyes
is like standing in front of divine.
O' my goodness
Will I ever be able to tell you
What your eyes do to me.
They fill me with peace.
They make me drop every wants
They take me to the other world.
May be to the heaven.
May be to the seventh.
It seems
you look directly at my soul.
Your eyes part of my whole.
I can't be anything
else in your gaze.
I can just be me.
Pure me,
true me
only me.
God bless your eyes

for being so pure
for being so kind on me
for being full of love
for being for me
God bless your eyes
for looking at me
the way you look at me....

Raghu Mahendru
Ludhiana, Punjab

Instagram ID- raghumahendru

1. Faith and trust in your actions are a must, but failure should also be an equal option. Sometimes when you encounter failure in life, just remember that it is only redirecting you towards a better opportunity. Remember as the wise say, that 'Failure is a blessing in disguise'. If one can embrace his/her failures in life, rather than sobbing about it, you will be a better person in the end.

2. Don't let your circumstances define who you are, as you are the sole creator of your destiny, believe in the faith of God & keep on doing your karma, keep following your passion & you will make a difference. Respect & explore the gifts you have been blessed with by the almighty. And never forget the mantra, to live and let live.

3. Understanding our skill set & passion in life could be quite a tricky thing, while it's said that a person that understands his passion, will never have to work & also heed either success or money in life. So sit, think and ask yourself what could you do better as a person, are you willing to make a name for yourself or just want to read others only. Each one of us has been given special gifts, it's the self-exploration, that is what needed.

Mohamed J. Faizal
Pondicherry

Instagram ID-5z_02_faizal

1. What's happening? Where are we?
In a world, where good people envy the
better.
Innocent minds hoping to see a miracle
that they know might never come.
Stop! Everyone, for a second.
Step back and tear everything away
that stops you from being you;
Because they are all nothing but
illusions,
Gifted to you by your past.

2. Shadow

Yes, he was alone
On a pitch dark night.
Far away he saw a saloon
From which came some light.

The day was bad,
As bad as it could have been.
That's why he was sad,
So sad he had ever been.

For he was an orphan
With his only friend indeed
Who was too, an orphan
That helped him in his need.

His one and only mate was he
That lost his life in a hurry;

Whilst he came, getting coffee
Got hit by a truck in fury.

He, who lost his mate all of a sudden
To share his grief has got no one;
Midnight 'twas and all he had was
burden.
Near the Saloon was a dark–black,
someone!

When he got near the light,
The someone, too, came in closer.
He felt his pants were tight
But chanted 'Don't be a loser'.

With his last step to the window;
Found, he, that the someone was
None but his own shadow,
And knew right then, why it was.

It came upfront, to give him
Strength and companionship;
To prove that "Always running is time"
And so, to build a new relationship.

Who knew the boy was so bright
That he caught it in the first sight.
Out came the tears from his eyes, from
a height;
For his only chap no more, with might.

Looking at his shadow
And thinking about the same,
Shed his final tears of sallow
For the friend with no name.

Then stood himself up, right
As the Sun did, too, the same;
Opened his eyes, looking straight

Through time when he'd have fame.

He took the first step
Of this now new life; with
His shadow, which alone he knows,
Schlep'd;
Following till the end, witnessing a myth.

Tamanna Mohapatra
Bhubneswar, Odisha

Instagram ID – _._tamannaaaa_._

Destination

The replaced .
The starry sky
Felt like a lie
No wonder
Why that thunder
Hold on..
Let me breathe
It's the screaming of never so silent me
The ocean of deep love and rooted
dedication
Changed to unfaithful and felt more like
destruction
My veins did not cope up with the
thought of being unloved
How can it stay still when things got
flustered
My eyes felt so heavy
I really don't know how to hold
Because it was the first ever time
I had to fight with my very own soul
Hands doesn't have strength to turn
into fist
That's the lost battle I was dealing with
For one last time I opened my eyes
Followed the path to the sea
It was there when I saw replica of me
Now, I got answers to all my query
The only question left was
Whether I deserve to get replaced ?
It was then I felt a beat

And it was there I knew the importance
of me
I might not play a role in your fantasy
story
But questioning myself for uh jerk won't
match my glory
You might change for several reason
But I am the one to decide
My destination.

Sonali Sharma
Mumbai, Maharastra

Instagram ID – sharma_writeups

1. When you Feel Defeated.

At point of life, there comes a time,
You feel dejected and loose your smile.
You search for a place to be alone,
You take a walk besides the shore.

You start hating yourself,
You start hating every one who's there
for help.
It is okay to face such situations in life,
After all they build up courage to make
us try!

It is definitely okay to cry hard or sob,
When you know to be alone, no one can
tend to stop.
You can get defeated in life to the
worst extent,
But when you hit to the lowest point,
your inner voice forces you to break the
crust.

2. Dream Comes True

We work throughout day and night.
Whole day busy schedule so tight.
We always try to get our work right.
While sleeping we relax a bit looking at
the sky.

We always wish to get our dreams
come true.

We fight with the odds any how.
For our dreams give us meaning to live.
Dreams when come true, give us a
sense of pride.

When we just keep on trying,
Whether we feel like giving up or dying.
That's where the journey takes the jerk,
And then the force drives you to the
top.

3. Morning Madness

Every dark night followed
By a sparkling ray of light.
Though nights may be depressed,
Every morning our soul tries to be
happy.

How ever alone we may be,
But every morning we see a ray of hope
All this seems nothing but a morning
madness
That entwines within us, pushing
ourselves to hope!

The only hope and spark of doing
something,
The belief of every dark night comes
with brightest dawn.
This is what keeps you going,
Even in the worst phases of life!

Vivek Marwaha
Ludhiana, Punjab

Instagram ID – vivek_marwaha

1. Trust your gut, do whatever you want. You don't own anybody anything. Take charge of your life because only you can make something out of it, nobody else will.

2. Be patient. Trust your process. There is nothing like loving your process to achieve something. Give your 100% and always remember that your result lies in your process.

3. Your failure may change your direction but can never let you stop from becoming what you are.

Baman Tadiwala
Gujrat

Instagram ID – b.a.m.a.n

World of my Dreams

I close my eyes,
and see a world –
where you're with me and every works
for us.
For you shine in your field
and I am the master of my own.
I hold your hand
and walk with pride.
Not for the world to see,
but for us to believe it's real.
My eyelids touch yours,
and I know you won't cry.
For you will see someone here
kissing your soul, oh dear!

I open my eyes,
and I know.
There is someone always better, you
know.
For I can only make you laugh,
He will be someone
who will keep your smile intact.
...and I will pray for that because I love
you.
If there is a next life,
Please, we two!

Prathna Das
Bhubneswar, Odisha

Instagram ID – prathna.das7

1. Choice

The choices that I once made
has engulfed into mistakes of lifetime
struggling to survive with those
mistakes
but it's painful to swim through gloom
the hands of time can't be turned back
the mistakes can't be undone
all that is left are the hard times
to be lived like a loop of heart aches,
piercing through the heart
reminding of what it could be
with more the days are passed by..
the feeling of guilt gets more
STRONGER
days turn into years and years into
decades
but seems to be right
hoping for a miracle to happen...
sitting near the river bank..
ain't no boat gonna sail
unless they are driven by a brave heart,
the howling winds wont even obey the
luck,
hard work and skills..
are needed to ride the sea horse
wide open the eyes
now it's time to ride
the faith is shining bright
and the believe is ready to guide
to sail the sea of high tides
and fight through the hurricanes

the path that leads to eternity
a happy place of peace,
lies far beyond the horizon ..
where self worth is determined,
and no soul is criticized.

2. Eyes of Devil

From the eyes of the devil
no one will be spared,
looks underneath the clothes
ready to eat the soul,
the unsatisfying hunger
will haunt every innocent body,
sympathy for none...
not even a child.
enjoys the scream
tears be the favourite poison
the devil is ready to wear the blood
society witnesses the horror
yet the law is bounded by the system,
blind folded is the court
corrupted is the system..
free is the society..
but fearful by the heart,
by shutting up the mouth
pretending to be fine,
ain't gonna kill the virus.
standing up against the wrong..
and empowering every being
teach them to empathize..
rather than sympathize
tell the society not to protect
but to respect every being
not just to learn gender equality in
books
but induce learning into the upbringing
raise the voice hell high

let the screams be heard
hiding behind the veils
ain't gonna bring justice
let people know the true meaning of
ITS NOT ME .. IT'S YOU..
it's not the matter of short dresses
or coming late to home..
it's not about attending parties
or living on streets..
it's not about being a boy or being a girl
it's the dirty thinking we are not safe
with..

Himanshu Leekha
Hisar, Haryana

Instagram ID– himanshuleekha001

1. One positive mind is better than thousand negative minds.

2. Whatever wrong happens in your life, you must take charge and fight like champion.

3. Success is not determined by your wealth, it is determined by your achievements.

Amandeep Verma
Chandigarh

1. Life is all about self pampering. Never get tired of loving yourself cause all these imperfections, fears, pessimistic attitude is just a myth. Life was given to you with a purpose, all you need to do is to find that purpose. A lot of obstacles may come en-route accomplishing success, but never let these obstacles stop you from questioning your identity and capability.

2. To reach to a certain height in life, you will seek lot of lessons and blessings on your way. Cherish the blessings but also do not forget the lessons.

3. Time is the most valuable asset you have, utilize it before it is too late. Because people who value time, life values them.

Dashmesh Saini
Bhopal, Madya Pradesh

Instagram ID- _aldhiyb

1. Stardust

The stardust in your heart
Is as blacked it can be
By your malevolence
Reckoning the proverb of hatreds
Befallen like a thunder on your past
Digging pathetic scars in your memory
Without any concerns of you.

The stardust which was known
To be the glitter of your pupils
Has lost its density of truth
Since when it turned black by your
malevolence
So in the end you had lost everything
Even your most beautiful gift
Known by gold in eyes,
Your stardust, sorry but you lost it, to
hatred.

2. I See You

I see you
Shining bright in the light
With gracefully sweetness aura
engulfing you
Goodies in my life, are by the reason
you tho
The deeper I go, this could be named as
love
"Even if I don't want, I acknowledge it as
love."

I see you
Erasing my darkness
Sealing my demon
Powering my soul
Presenting the light to me which lost
with hope
The confidence in abyss of grave
You are bringing up to me

I see you
Warming me up in my cold days
Moisturizing my dry lips with soft lips of
yours
The softness and life I felt from them
was my pioneer
I hadn't said you from start and you are
dying to listen
So finally I love you and loud as moon is
entity
And thank you for loving me even when I
am most despicable in world.

Lovie Matharoo
Ludhiana, Punjab

Instagram ID– loviematharoo

1. Its my battle, I am ready to fight
alone,
Today, without you I am ready to walk
on the flaming zone...
Its almost time time, I must stand with
head held high,
Even if you betray me, my love, I am not
gonna die....

2. Everyone is mudslinging behind my
back,
They consider me a dirty sack...
They don't know me what my life is all
about,
I am person who'll grow big from a mini
sprout...

Anjali Kashyap
Muzaffarpur, Bihar

Instagram ID – _scribbling__writer

1. What inspires you to work in-spite
of all the hurdles?", someone asked me.
I was quiet for a moment before I
started, "A sleep lover waking up early
morning,
A fun lover staying calm and quiet,
Staying alone being a company lover,
Skipping parties being a food lover,
Working late night knowing u won't be
granted an extra hour of sleep the next
morning,
Avoiding calls knowing the person next
would feel offended affecting their
friendship,
Sharing your life with just one person
though having many by side...
And many more such little things which
is quite common for the girl next door,
inspires me to work, to hold myself high,
to keep me motivated.....", I replied
taking necessary breaks

2. "What is inspiration?"
"A thought that simply helps you to
upgrade your potentials and work for a
better living standard."

3. "Why inspiration?"
"Just to make a clear decision when
your mind starts a debate with your
inner-self and you are stuck in between
ifs and buts ."

Priyanshi Mussadi
Kolkata, West Bengal

Instagram ID- _priyanshimussadi_

1. He is there to Bless

Giving up is easy
Staying throughout is Strength
Crying is pure
Not knowing why is Worst.
Being hurt is depressing
But Hurting is a Sin
Being Happy is courageous
For no reason is Scary
I stayed with him for long
I know leaving is Hard
Sometimes pain is good to bear
For I know he (God) is there to bless.

2. Hey dear!

Oh, so did I heard it right ?
You want to give up right?
So you are at your
'It's the end of the world for me'
Stage it seems...
And Suicide is the only way it seems...
Right?
But Wait,
No !
I won't say all those cheesy lines,
'Life is beautiful, live it , love it'
Because maybe it isn't ,
Maybe it is
Anyways doesn't matter

Maybe you don't need a solution to your
problems
Maybe you just need someone who can
listen to your problems
And say
" You're not alone in this."
Life is just like a coin babe
Good and bad are just words
Good times adds meaning to life
But bad times gives meaning to life

You are strong enough to face the
world
All you need is a warm hug
And a soul to listen to all your
What your mind is filled up with
For emotions are the most pure part of
your life
And when it fails to come out
You get an outburst
And your heart pushes you towards
depression and anxiety.

That's when you need a soul to trust
and say all that you feel,
At the end of day we all need a
comforting pillow to lay down
And for you,
I want to be the one
Because for me you were always the
one.

Shruti Tayal
Palwal, Haryana

Instagram ID–
spread_smile_shruti_skye

To My Inspiration

Light touches with hands
The only one who understands
Do whatever you can
Guess what?
I call you a real man!

All throughout my school years,
You've been my special teacher,
The day I saw you, I was awestruck,
Forgot all worries, You're my good luck,
Each day would be so dull,
If it doesn't start with your smile,
You showed me the path of success,
I remember your all motivated
conversations,
The lessons you taught were really the
best lessons,
You told me the difference b/w the right
and wrong,
I was a mystery box with puzzle pieces
inside,
Some of my pieces were broken,
But you sort them out and help me to
see,
The potential of greatness I've within,
Like a star you came in my life,
With Inspiring thoughts, you filled my
mind,
In everything I do, You serve me an
inspiration,

I truly thank you for being there in every situation,
Without you I can't even walk, how can I think to run,
In your need each second, Yes, it's your son.

Bikram Chowdhury
Malda, West Bengal

Facebook ID – @itsbikramchowdhury

1. Anymore

I don't think anymore
The things so fairy .
Oh thinking will do me no good ,
Rather rob me of my real vibes .

I don't love anymore
The stuffs outside of me
'Cause I know everything happens
within ,
Within the reach of my kingdom.

I don't feel anymore
The sensations with so damn a depth
'Cause it's no use to dig my own soul
Just to explore the pains under pains.

2. Path of Life

Full of moments, lively moments
Passing by in deep deep
And in untraceable nothingness,
Full of joys, full of pains
And of ever-changing chain of
incidents
Going on to form a life
Full of scars and of sweet experience ,
One day this very life will have
Its white changes on head
And its changes on skin and on face.
From that point this life will behold

Its path full of so called thorns
Which will seem then but full of roses.

3. To Thy Vicinity

I'll not go towards thee.
Still I'll come to thy vicinity.
'What ? How is it possible?'
Yea, it's possible in a way simple.
If you invest an infinite energy
To my feet and an end to my lethargy,
And forget the mortal rules of flesh,
And relish your waiting with earthly
pace,
I'll come to thy grace
For the World is round and fresh.
I'll walk opposite to thee
And the round World will lead me but to
thee...

Aaradhana Agarwal
Mumbai, Maharastra

Instagram ID – thepoeticmeee

New Perception of Life

'New perception, new life',
We are happy inside circumference
drawn by ourselves,
We say it loudly, again and again daily
once.
But are we really happy?
How can we?
The real happiness is locked deep in
heart,
It's key is handed over to Ego, who is
never soft,
Heart yearns for that real gem of life,
helplessly trying.
We are content inside the fake circle of
happiness and smile.
Life is full of sufferings.
There are more despair than hopes,
There are more tears than smiles,
There are more efforts than favourable
results,
There are more hurdles than easy going
paths,
There are more disappointments than
encouraging moments,
There are more Noes, than positive
Yeses.
Let decide!
Will we flow in the river of sufferings,
Or create our own island of happiness?
Make it a habit.
Find brightness in every gloomy
darkness.

Trace significance in all good or bed
events.
As a beautiful rainbow appears at the
junction of rain and sun,
Memorable life is built at the balance of
logic and emotion.
If finding dirt on others,
Make sure you're dust free.
As soiled glass makes vision blurred,
We clean it to get back clarity.
If situations seem confusing wipe the
fog settled on your heart,
When foggy glass makes you blind,
Clean it, then you're with right mind.
If people are seen two faced,
Change your outlook, it is outdated.
We change the broken glass if
showing objects in multiple parts.

Look at yourself before accusing else.
Be observant in choosing hearts for
love – growth.
Sow your seed of love in a fertile heart.
It will get nourishment, care and
attention
It will bloom and be a lovely flowering
plant with admiration.
Barren heart will destroy, crush and
burn your tender seed.
You would never trust again the
existence of love indeed.
Let emotions remain abstract and
temporary.
Don't stick to any one of these for long
adamantly.
Crimes are done due to an emotional
outburst with vile intention,
Due to an inability of handling extreme
of any specific emotion.

How to prevent hearts sinking deep into
the quagmire I thought a lot and found a
solution as a responsible writer.
Let Love to be loved,
Friendship to be befriended,
Hate to be hated.
I am sure, peace can be prevailed,
Negativity can be omitted,
Let stop judging human, none is meant
to be bitterly hated.
Feelings are in abundance,
So cherish their abstractness.
Don't measure it as it leads to ugly
comparison.
Don't demand it as we all will lose in
oblivion.
These are eternal, balancing the
universe.
Feel blessed if feel their presence,
Even in fraction, with and around us.
Every beginning is meant to end surely
Let's start a task by deciding deadline
firmly.
If you make heart ready to face the day
When you'll move to some other bay,
You can enjoy every bit of the task till
completion,
Unaffected to any destiny, your next
plan is ready for action.
There is no loss– gain if you live your
life like this
You'll always be in win – win situation
without a miss.

Geetanshi Muttreja
Sonipat, Haryana

1. Life is like a Tunnel

One day I was fiddling through life and the other day I realized there was nothing good to be extracted from it. Deep down a shallow tunnel exists where light does go inside but doesn't pass through since it gets hurdled by darkness from the other side. The fierce darkness proves to be more stronger than the light that was actually making its way to somewhere good. However, neither of them wants either of them to win. With all their force they push one another to let the other one go out. 'Ughh!' I groaned, perhaps couldn't bear this tug of war anymore and somehow tried to break the tunnel. Survival of one never seemed to happen. To settle this war of conflict I had to emerge a beam of inspiration that traverses in between both for I could see no other way to escape it.

2. Inspiration

Begins from within
The invention of new creation
Even to move the mountains
And through every thick and thin
Nostalgia may hit you hard
While you wishing upon a star
You may lower every bar
Success is the only pick out

Indeed in this journey
You are your own scout
Adorned with your persistence is your
hope
Because when chips are down
You need inspiration to cope
Hand in hand with innovation
One can reach the wonders
Torments for sure would occur
But nothing can be as huge as your
inspiration to muster
Wear it as your crown
As if you own it with renown...

Lavi Sha
Ludhiana, Punjab

Instagram ID- lavi_sha_233

1. Roadside kid

I had a bad day in office, my boss had said some words like you have changed, not focusing on your work and making mistakes from past fifteen or thirty days, which you have never made before. And yeah I did. I was out of my mind. My brain was seriously somewhere else while working. I was walking on the road with all the incidents of today running on repeat in my mind. Am I a failure, am I not responsible, am I a looser or a fool. Am I not going anywhere, am I not growing up. Why all this is happening. I had no clue. I was just so fed up.

Fed-up with last night conversation of me with a friend which ended up with a breakup. Fed-up with no career plan of what to do next. Half of my mind was in my father's health. All this on repeat on loop running in my mind. I was in a crowd area, where no one can recognize others, and my tears roll out, had a burning headache. I was crying and walking at one side of the road.

This kid from left side came with his baggage of plastic waste, not even wearing socks in this freezing cold, hardly have any money, he was about six years old. I was just about to pass him through a side, he turned back and smile.

Then he laughed at me, not as in annoying but as like kids, for no reason. I was surprised for a moment. And envying the kid in the other moment. And enjoying and smiling with him in the other.

Sometimes we think there's only us who are suffering.

What we never understand is, suffering is just an exam to make us more strong. From that day I stopped crying and complaining about life.

2. It's not that you can't count on every one.

Its that you shouldn't need to count on every one.

3. Once in school time a question in chit game was asked from me ...
What's the meaning of hard work?
I was numb, had no answer...
Now I want to make my life be the answer of it...

Muskan Goel
Hazaribagh, Jharkhand

Instagram ID – goel_muskan22

1. Life is actually all about womb to
tomb
But its you who must decide your own
destiny
Be a model who design her own dress.
Or a beautiful flower of valley or a river.
Go on a voyage if you can't be a
captain be in crew.

If its hard to find a road become your
own trail.
Shine bright. If you can't be a sun then
be your own lamp.
Be a decider don't let man to cage your
dreams.
Even When all hope is lost, you must
stand tall.
When all others retreat, you must
prevail.
You are the conscience inside your
head.
You create your own destiny.
Because everyone is unique in this
world.

2. In this life, you will somewhere at
some time meet someone special. Who
will always say the right word at the
right moment. But when the time comes
for the action you will know.

So believe in action not in words.

3. Dear Stranger

Cheating can never be a reason it is an excuse to come out of something you are bored of because there is no more spark you can feel in it and yet you were bound because of your reasons. So let it just go rather than cheating and devastating someone who were once more than someone to you.

Danica Rayen
Tamil Nadu

Instagram ID – vrayen8998

1. "There's still time
To wake your confidence
To take your challenges
To make your life cheerful
Never step back."

2. "Re-Born is possible
    when you face betrayals frequently
but still doing good to all."

3. "When patience roses in your life ,
the word change will arose."

Sabi Shaikh
Hyderabad

Instagram ID– thesabishaikh

Extraordinary life

Passion, a small seven letter word. Some spend their entire lives finding their passion while the others make their life because they were lucky enough to find their passion. Passion is what separates the extraordinary from the ordinary. It can be acting, music, or it can be just your normal desk job but if you do it with passion, then there is a big possibility that you'll go places. Living without being passionate about something is like living without actually living.

Growing up in a Mumbai surrounded by poverty wasn't really easy. You either perish in poverty like most people do or you end up being that one in a million who makes it out to see the light. This journey towards light is never simple but that wild passion in you makes this journey worthwhile. I wasn't really good with my academics so I knew that being a doctor or a scientist was out of the question. I was good in Cricket though but was asked to leave the cricket academy as my parents couldn't really afford the fees. So, with a heavy heart I kept my Bat aside making a promise to myself that this will never happen to my children.

I was heartbroken but life goes on and like it or not you have to keep walking.

My life was pretty ordinary until the day I entered a poetry writing completion in school and won the first prize. I thought it was a fluke but as time flew by and I grew up, I had discovered that I had a flair for writing. I had discovered my Passion.

I had completed my academic years and had stepped into the corporate life. Heaped with responsibilities I kept walking while I still kept scribbling stories here and there. Money was important but I just didn't want to end up being another rat in the race. Amid-st all the chaos that life offered, I found peace in writing. It made me happy like nothing ever could. Writing random stories about love and life kept me going. Love, because when you fall in love it is always beautiful and life because eventually life happens and people walk away.

Surrounded by the chaos of life and a few shattered dreams I decided that life can't go on like this anymore. Remember the promise that I had made to myself while I bid farewell to my cricket academy? I took my chance and typed my boss a resignation email. I grabbed my pen, opened my heart and I wrote about our hypocrite society. I spoke about love, I went against caste and said it's wrong to keep religion above love. People applauded and my debut novel, Via Delhi – A twisted tale of love got me recognized even by Google. My Name is Sabi Shaikh who will keep his promise. I followed my passion and this is how I found the extraordinary from my ordinary life.

Bios of Writers

Sanjana Sankhyan

Sanjana Sankhyan is a B.com student. She's 19 years old and started writing when she was 16. Although not a frequent writer, she's finds it very therapeutic.

She also loves to explore music, food binge while watching new shows and movies. She has a old school and hopeless romantic kind of personality, also, believes in spreading love and kindness.

Mankaran Singh

Mankaran Singh is a civil engineer by profession. He did his graduation from Thapar University, Patiala and is currently working as JE in Municipal Corporation, Ludhiana.

Apart from the job, he is quick-witted and wannabe person. He loves to travel and dreams to experience different type of cuisines around the world.

Mankaran and Chetan(Compiler) are childhood friends

Suryansh S.

Suryansh hails from the city of Gwalior, Madhya Pradesh. A teenager with loads of talents & aims above the sky. A complete artist : Writer, Memer, Poet, Author, Actor, Intern @ www.artofzindagi.com & a National Karate Player.

Vishal Tekade

Vishal Tekade hails from Nagpur, he is currently pursuing his studies in business administration. He aspires to be a motivational speaker and is also passionate about writing.
His debut book, 'Reborn Within', is releasing this year.

Kaandeeban Mohanraj

Kaandeeban M, a 20-year-old medico, writer, blogger, violinist from Karaikal, Puducherry. He is studying medicine in IGMCRI, Puducherry. Unlike others, his writing journey started from a four-lined handwriting notebook to blogs. He desired to help budding writers and so he together with his buddies formed a platform called 'infinitemaxims'. He is hooked on his forthcoming first novel, but he will always be a helping hand at anytime.

Kanak Lata Sharma

Kanak Lata Sharma, now eighteen, grew up in Ghazipur, Uttar Pradesh and is currently pursuing her bachelors in commerce.
Kanak lata Sharma is a writer of musings, sipper of Tea, and addict of anything story and poem. Having learned life while exploring the edges of society, it's through storytelling she finds her footing in the world-as a mom, sister and citizen.

Mona Dokania

Mona Dokania, holding a Master's degree in Economics and pursuing Company secretary, is a writer and poet by heart, raised in Gurugram. 24 year old dedicates her soul to poetry with a belief in the healing power of prowess poems and loves to paint Archaic Rhymes.

Priyanka Vegda

Priyanka Vegda is a junior artist in film industry and freelance model since 7 years. My age is 26 year old. A dedicated writer, blogger, poet, story teller, fashion addict, and a spiritual soul.
You can connect with her via –
Facebook– priyanka vegda
Instagram I'd – priyanka_vegda and writing Id – ansunisi.

Varsha Saxena

Varsha Saxena hails from the City of Nawabs. She is the daughter of a brave soul, her mother. She has completed her graduation from CSJM University, Kanpur. She adores Robin Sharma and his words, "Greatness comes from the beginning of something that doesn't end with you". She pens in Hindi, Urdu and English. Her ink flows around poetries, couplets, nazms and stories. Her words crown her pain. She caters to all the painful beings out there.

Mohamed Faizal

Mohamed Faizal J is a 20 yr old medico from Puducherry's IGMC&RI. He completed his middle school at Cauvery Public School, Karaikal and finished his high school at Jawahar Navodaya Vidyalaya, Karaikal (JNVK). He thinks random stuffs and likes writing it up and puts up quotes and poems that he wrote, on his social account. He loves listening to people more and being their blanket of comfort.

He loves to be around his friends and loved ones. He is of the idea that life is all about surprises (no matter the size of the surprise). And...who doesn't love surprises!?

Sonali Sharma

Sonali Sharma, a young girl from a small town, who wishes to achieve great heights and make her parents feel proud. She wishes to be a good and generous person. She's currently pursuing Bachelor's degree in Accounting and Finance, along with that she's pursuing ICWA.

She's a great Book lover and passionate to write! One day, she wishes to be a known author. She seeks for new opportunities to explore the world and tries, even the smallest way to help out the society. She has been the co-author of quite a few anthologies and is an author of one book. She works with NGO as spending time and teaching small and needy kids, is where she finds happiness.

You can reach her at sonalisharmasunil@gmail.com

Areeba Ashraf

Areeba Ashraf (writer) is from Sitapur, Uttar Pradesh. She is a student and a writer of a blissful language which is English. She write long form poetry, two liners and articles. Reading, writing, travelling and exploring new things creates the essence of her life.

Connect with Areeba via–
Facebook – Areeba Ashraf
Instagram– @tanyaashraf123

Prathna Das

Prathna is from Bhubaneswar an entrepreneur with a postgraduate of mass communication degree and a business administration graduate. She runs her own company. Writing is her obsession and wants to make a difference with her writing.

Point of contact-
prathna.das7
(Instagram)

Vivek Marwaha

Vivek Marwaha is 20 years old and is a native of Ludhiana. He is a B.Com student and is interested in the business and corporate world. He wants to make a big impact on business someday and aspires to write and publish his own business books. Openness to experience is his core strength. He believes that, 'A person's real competition is no one else, but himself'.

Social media Handle
Instagram= vivek_marwaha

Dashmesh Saini

Dashmesh saini belongs from the kingdoms of lakes, Bhopal.
He wants to be a poet and novelist and for now he address himself as a wannabe poet. He believes that learning is a continuous process. Every day is a opportunity to learn something new.

Priya Nayer

Priya Nayer is a poetess and a flautist. She loves to practice and teach accountancy. She has done her schooling from Girls' High College, Prayagraj and is pursuing graduation from University of Allahabad.

Baman Tadiwala

Baman Tadiwala hails from Vadodara, Gujrat. Being an author of 5 books, Baman holds strong passion towards writing. Graduated from Dharmsinh Desai University as Chemical Engineer, he is currently pursuing his masters in Canada.

Shruti Tayal

Shruti Tayal is brought up in Palwal, Haryana. She is 18 years old. Currently, she is pursuing her graduation in physics.

She started writing almost two years ago to follow her instincts and now she traps her readers with her words. She is a true example of determinant and hard working. She has worked in many anthologies as a co-author, promoter, and manager. Besides writing, she loves to read & review novels, cooking, etc. She wishes to be a novelist someday.

You can connect with her via:
Instagram: @spread_smile_shruti_skye

Bikram Chowdhury

Bikram Chowdhury is a passionate student of Literature, aspiring writer, optimist & a fun-maker born in a beautiful town, Malda, West Bengal. Along with writing, twenty years-old spiritualist Bikram loves music & movies too.

Aaradhana Agarwal

Aaradhana Agarwal has been penning her emotions since her school going days. A literary family background and Masters in English literature have developed her interest in writing poems, stories and articles. She is a keen observer and sharp thinker and doesn't live in past. She admits situations in its reality without any beautiful coating of falsehood and reveals the hard core truth in her creations.
Books – True love (Co – author)
          Tangible Abstracts (Author)

Insta– @thepoeticmeee

Geetanshi Muttreja

Geetanshi Muttreja, an avid reader turned author, born on June 7, 1999 is a computer science student and a published writer best known for her writing, acting and singing skills.
Poetry writing for her is a deep passion and her poetries depict realities in life coupled with spirituality in love and longings.

Anjali Kashyap

Born in Muzaffarpur, Bihar, Anjali Kashyap comes from joint family background and an amazing friend circle has always inspired her to write about relationships and expectations. She is interested in writing poetry and prose both in Hindi and English. Her work generally express feelings which are very common in existence but are least expressed. She is very passionate about writing and wants to write for the common people. It's easy to understand her work beautifully scripted in simple language.
Check out her Instagram page- @_scribbling__writer

Kriti Sood

Kriti Sood was born and brought up in Ludhiana. She is a law graduate from Panjab university, writer, poet and a lyricist. She loves cooking and singing.
You can get in touch with her-
Insta- @ksood036
YouTube Channel- Kav-E-Kriti.

Amandeep Verma

Amandeep Verma belongs to Chandigarh. She is a law graduate and currently pursuing her masters.

She has a charismatic personality and always urges to look on the bright side of life. This anthology is compiled by her best friend-classmate, that's the motivation behind her piece of work.

Tamanna Mohapatra

Tamanna is from Bhubaneswar, Odisha. She is a happy go lucky person with a lot of enthusiasm to write about different aspect of life and society. She wants to be a versatile writer and also stress upon the power of poems to trigger emotions. She dreams to be pilot and would also love to continue writing.

Apart from creative writing, she loves to dance and is also good in debating and painting. She hopes that with her skills she could surely be an asset for the world.

Himanshu Leekha

Himanshu Leekha holds a master degree in law. He is passionate about cooking, travelling, and loves to write in his free time.
23-year old Himanshu determines to become a Judge one day. You can connect with him—

Instagram Id— @himanshuleekha001

Anuj Arjun

Anuj hails from Roorkee, Uttarakand. He completed his graduation in B.tech and got his dream job as in Application engineer in IIT, Roorkee. Along with it, he is an author of five books –
My Blind Father
Life
Zindagi Agar Gulzar Hoti
Kabir... and other stories, and
Jad aur Chetan.

You can get in touch with him—
Facebook— @writeranujfamily
Twitter— @anujarjun11

Raghu Mahendru

Raghu Mahendru is a final year engineering student in the ECE domain. A native of Ludhiana. Apart from academics, he is an aspiring leader and has also served as the Convenor of IETEGNDEC Students Forum. He is a moviegoer and also operates his blogs on WordPress and Insta. He loves to research emerging technologies and practices, both in his core field and also other professions. He visions to grow as a social media influencer in future. Connect with Raghu via his:

Instagram ID: raghumahendru

Muskan Goel

Muskan Goel resides in Hazaribagh, Jharkhand. She has completed her Graduation and now pursuing Masters. She is a little confused don't know what path to take the one less walked or one taken by many. Reading has always been part of her life as it provides solace to her. Writing is something that makes her happy and is an important part of her life. Traveller by heart but not seen the world so far.

Sakshi Arora

Sakshi Arora has post graduated in English Literature and holds a diploma in French language. She is a poet, a Verbal, Communication and Personality Development trainer.

For her, poetry is the way to find emotional catharsis. She believes that poetry sheds a light on the world and provides the best way to express yourself and understand others.

You can connect with her via email: asakshi465@gmail.com

Priyanshi Mussadi

Priyanshi Mussadi is a B.Com Student who has keen interest in writing and has been studying literature for quite a long time.

For her, Writing is a therapy by which she pampers her thoughts into words.

Apart from writing , she even likes cooking and exploring new people and their experiences about life.

You can get to know about her social life through:

Facebook: @priyanshi.mussadi

Shubham Singh

Shubham Singh is a poet, philosopher, mentor and career counselor. He helps people find their purpose in life. Breathing Secrets is his first book. He lives in Prayagraj, and loves doing maths.

You can reach out to him on Facebook, Twitter and Instagram @livesimpicite or drop a mail at livesimplicite@gmail.com

Rimjhim Chandrakant

Rimjhim Chandrakant has been writing since she was 9-years old. A student of tenth grade, she helps people unfold life's unseen phases through her writings. She lives in Prayagraj and believes the power of pen can change the world. She is the most amazing and youngest contributor of this anthology.

Sunita Jash

Sunita Jash is a writer, blogger and trans-creator from Kolkata. She works for School Education Department (West Bengal) and is pursuing her Master's in English Literature. Apart from being passionate about folk art and culture of India, she is a Kathak dancer who discovers life in an optimistic and artistic way.

To connect with Sunita, email: jashsunita@gmail.com

Anjali Jha

Anjali Jha is from a small village of Darbhanga district of Bihar. She is a poet, reviewer and blogger. Apart from being featured in more than eighty books, she has also compiled five anthologies. She has worked with different organizations like TSM and Radio Vrishti.

You can contact her on
Facebook– Anjali Jha
Instagram– anjalikumarijha

Yasmin Khan

Yasmin Khan is from Pondicherry and believes that writing has kept her alive. Her writings mostly touches subjects like love, heart-breaks and high feels.
She is a public speaker and posts her writings on Instagram @dark_artist _ .
_

Danica Rayen

Danica Rayen is an Aeronautical Engineer from Chennai. She loves her career as well as passionate about expressing her thoughts into words... She has participated nearly 15 anthologies and presently compiling her first book "Drive of Orenda" .You can contact her at @vrayen8998(insta ID)

Lavisha

Lavisha (pen name Lavi Sha) is from Ludhiana, Punjab. She holds a graduate degree in commerce. She don't know where her flair for writing came up from, might be in her genes or pen became her best friend. She believes in unbelievable, unrealistic, impossible, and the power of universe .

Family and her friends are on her priority list. And her favourite writings which she had also recited in a college fest is Robert Frost's poem "the woods are lovely dark and deep, but I have promises to keep and a miles to go before I sleep" – "stopping by woods on a snowy evening", are her inspiration.

She believes in writing the most. She adores, 'One can write half truth but one can never write a total lie.'

Rajat Joshi

Rajat Joshi is a lawyer by profession but poet by passion. He hails from the city of Hoshiarpur. Apart from writing, he has an interest for dancing and travelling.

Rajat is quite known in the city for his quick witted attitude and of course for his beautiful poetries.

You can connect with via–
Instagram– _darkershade_

Lovie Matharoo

Lovie Matharoo belongs to, 'Manchester of India' – Ludhiana. He completed his graduation in commerce and currently pursuing his Masters. He is passionate about singing, writing lyrics, and has released many single tracks which are available on Youtube.

Get to know more about Lovie via-
Instagram- loviematharoo
Youtube Channel- Lovi Matharoo

Sabi Shaikh

A Mumbaikar at heart with Hyderabadi soul. Sabi Shaikh is the author of books Via Delhi and Knocked Out. He has also featured in various other poem and short story anthology. Apart from writing, Sabi is also very passionate about fitness.
He is also a certified Fitness Trainer and a Nutritionist. He loves travelling to new places and watching movies whenever he can. Sabi lives his life by the quote, "Winner don't do different things, they do things differently."

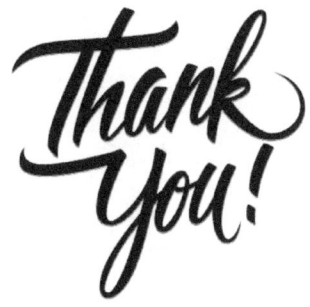